Each of us by ourselves is nobody. It is only when somebody interfaces with other somebodies that we all become somebody.

—James Boggs

Saying you have an ideology is saying you are one thing. I don't think any of us are one thing. I try to combine ideas. If I had to call myself anything, I'd call myself a community activist and a political thinker.

—Grace Lee Boggs

TO THE NEXT GENERATION OF YOUNG ACTIVISTS AND CHANGEMAKERS
—S.Y.S., M.M., and L.B.

Acknowledgments

Thank you so much to Grace Lee Boggs, James Boggs, Jane Jeong Trenka, Scott Kurashige, and Carol Hinz and everyone at Lerner. Huge thanks to my wonderful circle of friends and colleagues—too many to list, but you know who you are—who have been so supportive of my path as a writer and reader and who inspire me every day with their creativity, humor, brilliance, and dedication to a better world. Biggest thanks go to fearless coauthor Mélina Mangal, an incredible writer and advocate, and the person who has brought so much knowledge, beauty, skill, history, and power to this book project. I am so fortunate to get to learn alongside her!
—S.Y.S.

A sincere thank-you to Donald Boggs for sharing time, stories, and insights into his father's life. Deep gratitude and respect to Shea Howell, Dr. Stephen Ward, and Kimberly Sherobbi of the Boggs Center, for welcoming me to Detroit and sharing information, recollections, and movement updates. Thanks also to Rich Feldman for connecting me; and to Elizabeth, Stefanie, Paul, and the other librarians and assistants at Reuther Library, Wayne State University. Carol, Danielle, and the rest of the Lerner team, thank you for your thoughtful and diligent work to bring this book to young readers, and to Leslie Barlow for the beautiful illustrations. Thank you, Sun Yung, for inviting me to work with you on this amazing biographical journey, and for tirelessly championing the work of James and Grace Lee Boggs.
—M.M.

My sincere and deepest gratitude to Grace Lee Boggs and James Boggs, whose tireless work and radical love inspired this project. Thank you Sun Yung Shin and Mélina Mangal for entrusting me with the visual language of this story—I am honored to bring your words to life. Special thanks to Danielle Carnito and Carol Hinz for your encouragement and trust throughout this entire process, and to Suriya Khuth and Mel Owens for research support. Endless gratitude to my parents, ancestors, friends, family, and community of fellow artists, mentors, educators, and students, whose voices and stories echo through everything I create.
—L.B.

Carolrhoda Books®
An imprint of Lerner Publishing Group, Inc.
241 First Avenue North
Minneapolis, MN 55401 USA

For reading levels and more information, look up this title at www.lernerbooks.com.

Photo credits: courtesy of James and Grace Lee Boggs Foundation, p. 40. Illustration reference photos: James and Grace Lee Boggs Foundation, pp. 19, 24; Bettmann/Getty, pp. 20, 31 (Nkrumah); John Springer Collection/Corbis/Getty Images, p. 31 (Dee); Universal History Archive/Getty Images, p. 31 (Russell); Davis Freeman (Davis).

Designed by Danielle Carnito.
Main body text set in ITC Franklin Gothic Std.
Typeface provided by International Typeface Corporation.
The illustrations in this book were created with oil and acrylic paint, ink, thread, and textiles.

Library of Congress Cataloging-in-Publication Data

Names: Shin, Sun Yung, author. | Mangal, Mélina, author. | Barlow, Leslie, 1989- illustrator.
Title: Revolutions are made of love : the story of James Boggs and Grace Lee Boggs / Sun Yung Shin and Mélina Mangal ; illustrated by Leslie Barlow.
Description: Minneapolis : Carolrhoda Books, [2025] | Audience term: Children | Audience: Ages 7-11. | Audience: Grades 4-6. | Summary: A collection of poems introducing the lives and ideas of James Boggs and Grace Lee Boggs, revolutionary activists who worked together to build a better future for all.
Identifiers: LCCN 2024048411 (print) | LCCN 2024048412 (ebook) | ISBN 9798765611524 (library binding) | ISBN 9798765673256 (epub)
Subjects: LCSH: Boggs, James—Juvenile poetry. | Boggs, Grace Lee—Juvenile poetry. | Children's poetry, American. | CYAC: Boggs, James—Poetry. | Boggs, Grace Lee—Poetry. | Reformers—Poetry. | American poetry. | LCGFT: Biographical poetry. | Picture books.
Classification: LCC PS3619.H575 R48 2025 (print) | LCC PS3619.H575 (ebook) | DDC 811/.6—dc23/eng/20250129

LC record available at https://lccn.loc.gov/2024048411
LC ebook record available at https://lccn.loc.gov/2024048412

Manufactured in the United States of America
1-1011933-51774-5/23/2025

REVOLUTIONS ARE MADE OF LOVE

The Story of James Boggs *and* Grace Lee Boggs

Poems by
SUN YUNG SHIN *and* MÉLINA MANGAL

Paintings by
LESLIE BARLOW

CAROLRHODA BOOKS
Minneapolis

You don't choose the times you live in, but you do choose who you want to be and how you ought to think.

—Grace Lee Boggs

CONTENTS

1915: Providence, Rhode Island / 4
1919: Marion Junction, Alabama / 5
The Only Chinese American Family in Their Neighborhood / 6
"No Time to Be Bored" / 7
They Called Her a Foreigner / 8
Learning / 10
Higher Education / 12
Riding the Rails / 14
Whites Only / 15
Labor / 16
Fighting for Fair Housing / 18
A Purpose / 20
Movement / 22
Fearless / 24
Grace and James / 26
In Love and Struggle / 29
Dialectical Conversation / 29
Also Known As / 30
Revolution / 32
New Dreams for the Twenty-First Century / 32
Rebuilding Our Cities / 34
Being Part of the Solution / 35
What Kind of World Do We Want? / 36

NOTES FROM SUN YUNG SHIN / 38
NOTES FROM MÉLINA MANGAL / 38
NOTES FROM LESLIE BARLOW / 39
GLOSSARY / 40
QUOTATION SOURCES / 41
SELECTED BIBLIOGRAPHY / 41

1915: PROVIDENCE, RHODE ISLAND

The girl was born with two first names:
the American name *Grace*
and the Chinese name 玉平 (*Yuk Ping*),
which means "Jade Peace."
She had one sister
and five brothers,
a mother,
and a father.

Her family lived
above her father's bustling restaurant,
and when Grace would cry about something,
the waiters mocked her
and said,
"She's only a girl,"
but to Grace it was no laughing matter.

1919: MARION JUNCTION, ALABAMA

James came
into this world,
the youngest
of Leila and Ernest's four kids.
They were live-in workers for
a white couple,
Dr. Donald and Miz Elvie.
Ernest repaired machines
for the farm,
and Leila worked
as a domestic—
a servant in the home.

Folks in Europe
were agreeing to end
the war of all wars,
and a pandemic
spread flu and fear.
Closer to home,
fabric mills
consumed cotton for cloth.

Dallas County, Alabama,
produced a powerful proportion
of the puffy white plant
picked by people
like Big Ma,
James's great-grandmother
who'd been enslaved.

Too often
the Ku Klux Klan
would lynch a Black man
to keep Black people
"in their place."

Marion Junction,
James's birthplace,
crossroads
of Jim Crow and cotton.

THE ONLY CHINESE AMERICAN FAMILY IN THEIR NEIGHBORHOOD

Grace's father dreamed
of opening a Chin Lee Restaurant on Broadway,
and when Grace was eight,
they moved to New York City
so he could do just that.

He found some land where he could build a house
in the Jackson Heights neighborhood of Queens,
but he could not buy it
directly, as his own.
He had to make the purchase
in the name of his Irish contractor
because of racism.

Grace's mother, father,
sister, and brothers
lived bright and busy.
Surrounded
by white families
on all sides,
they lived and grew.

"NO TIME TO BE BORED"

All James wanted to do
was meet his friends,
but the animals
needed tending,
the icebox pan
needed emptying,
the night's ashes
needed to be carted away.
So many chores to do
before he could finally play.
He ran errands
to get items at the store.
He helped care for Big Ma.
He picked cotton,
minding the sharp, dry bolls
that pricked his fingers.
But when he picked blackberries,
he didn't mind
the thorns
or the hornets
or the snakes
that hid near the bushes.
A nickel a quart
in his berry-stained hands
made him feel
like he owned the world.

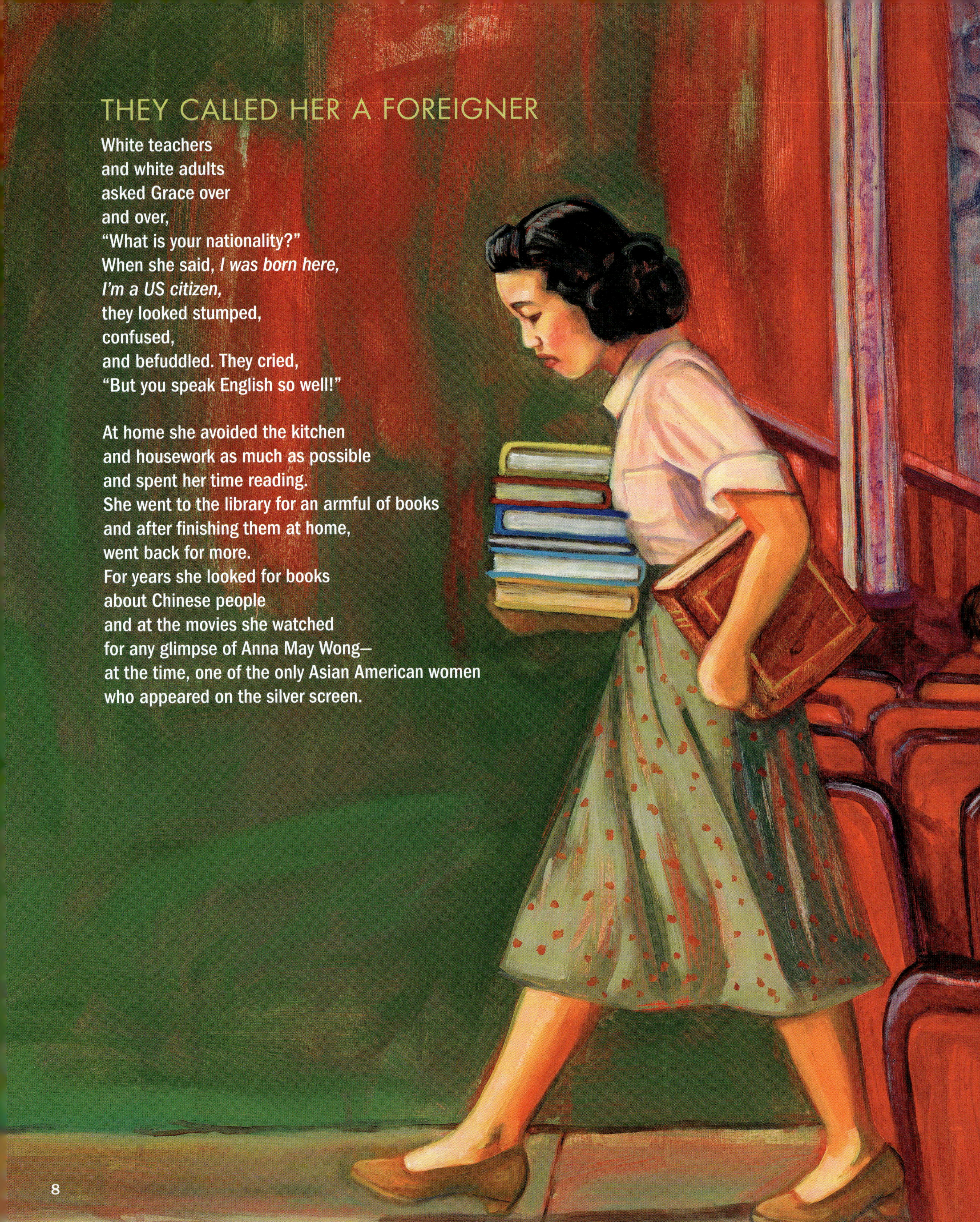

THEY CALLED HER A FOREIGNER

White teachers
and white adults
asked Grace over
and over,
"What is your nationality?"
When she said, *I was born here,*
I'm a US citizen,
they looked stumped,
confused,
and befuddled. They cried,
"But you speak English so well!"

At home she avoided the kitchen
and housework as much as possible
and spent her time reading.
She went to the library for an armful of books
and after finishing them at home,
went back for more.
For years she looked for books
about Chinese people
and at the movies she watched
for any glimpse of Anna May Wong—
at the time, one of the only Asian American women
who appeared on the silver screen.

LEARNING

James watched
his father's fingers fix
farm machines:
plows, presses, tractors.
He'd pounded
hot iron
as a blacksmith
and shoveled ore
as a miner.
Working with his hands
made him a man.

Mama Leila could not read
or write,
but she knew the right
thing for James was to
get an education.

"Baby, you do whatever
makes you happy in life.
Try to do something
that makes the world
a little better,"
she told him.

Big Ma shared
her strength
and stories
and spirituals
that soothed James's soul,
especially when his father died.
James was eight years old.

She recollected too
the cruel treatment
she'd lived through
during slavery times.

She taught James
about how history
shifts and changes,
how slavery ended
through struggle—
not because
slaveholders
wanted to
"free" the people.

Miz Elvie
paid his train fare
to school each day,
saved newspapers
and books
just for James
to read.
He never
stopped.

Elders asked James
to read letters
from sons and daughters
who'd fled Alabama.
So James learned
about jobs and life up North.
He penned responses
sharing news of daily life,
becoming the community scribe.

James moved in with Grandma Bettie
in Bessemer
to continue his schooling at
Paul Laurence Dunbar High School.

Studying with educators
from Talladega, Tuskegee, and Fisk,
James loved
Black History Week
when he'd finally hear
about the accomplishments
and struggles
of Black people,
filling him
with pride.

HIGHER EDUCATION

Grace was a brilliant student.
Skipped ahead in grade school,
she graduated eighth grade
before she turned twelve.
At just sixteen years old,
she went to Barnard College,
one of three students of color.

In 1933, while Hitler
rose to power in Europe
Grace asked herself hard questions
about good and evil,
truth and falsehoods,
and the meaning of life.
She dropped most of her classes
and sat in on courses in philosophy,
knowing that she had to learn
to think for herself.

After college,
Grace had a degree in philosophy,
could use a typewriter
and write in shorthand,
but not one
white person
would give her
a job
at an office
or a department store.

Most companies
would come right out
and say,
"We don't hire
Orientals."
Unemployed, she was lucky
to hear of a scholarship for
Chinese students
at Bryn Mawr College.

Accepted into the philosophy department,
Grace headed to the campus
in Pennsylvania
that spread across acres
of green rolling hills,
thick with trees.

RIDING THE RAILS

Graduating from high school
was a turning point for James
and his friend Joe.
Just as the seasons
know when it's time to change,
James knew it was time
to leave Alabama.

When you've got nothing,
it ain't nothing
to hop a train
and leave
the lynching
and the segregation
and the step-aside-when-a-white-person's
on-the-sidewalk.

No extra clothes.
No extra shoes
or money
or food.

James and Joe traveled
cross-country
along with thousands
of others
searching for jobs.

At new towns,
kind strangers
gave out ham hocks and cabbage
when hunger forced James and Joe
to knock on doors.

They were always looking out.
Railroad yard detectives and cops
would try to steal hobos away
to work on farms
without pay.

Riding in freezing cold boxcars,
James nearly lost
his left foot
to frostbite.

Ashes from the engines
temporarily
blinded James
and disqualified him
permanently
from going to war.

WHITES ONLY

It was the middle of the 1930s
on a train chugging
from Ohio
east to New York.
Grace rode in a "regular coach"
Whites Only,
as the train
and its segregated cars of passengers
crossed over the Ohio River,
the invisible line
between the North and South.

A conductor approached
Grace, asked her
to move
to the Jim Crow car.
She moved.

Later the conductor returned,
saying he made
a mistake and
she could move back
to the regular coach.

Grace, among the Black travelers,
going the same direction,
decided
not to move.
She stayed with the people
being treated
like second-class citizens.
Grace never forgot
that America treated her better
because she wasn't Black.
She'd made
her choice.

LABOR

James knew work.
He'd picked cotton in Alabama,
harvested hops in Washington,
cut ice in Minnesota.
He followed
his uncles and brothers
to Detroit,
home of the automotive industry,
but he could not get hired.

When the US entered
World War II,
Detroit became
the "arsenal of democracy"
and James finally got a job
in a factory.

At first, James worked
in the foundry—
one of the only
places Black men *could* work.

War production
turned James into
one of the first
Black materials handlers:
standing, pulling, turning,
gloved hands hoisting
plates of steel,
unloading shafts,
pushing wagons
heavy with sheet metal rolls
7 days a week
10 hours a day.

But in the factory
James also learned about unions—
made of members
who meet
and vote
and plan
and study
and strike
when workers
are underpaid
or injured,
overworked or sick,
when the factory floor
is unsafe,
understaffed,
unfair.

James joined
the United Auto Workers
and began writing
for the *Citadel*, the union paper.

He was now
an autoworker
and a union member,
a leader
and a writer,
a labor activist.

FIGHTING FOR FAIR HOUSING

In June 1940, done with Bryn Mawr,
Grace wanted a change,
needed a new challenge
for her restless mind.
With only one suitcase and a few dollars,
she boarded a train
to a new place
where she had no friends or family.
In the big Midwestern city of Chicago,
where racist segregation
kept the best
apartments, homes,
jobs,
and schools
for white families.

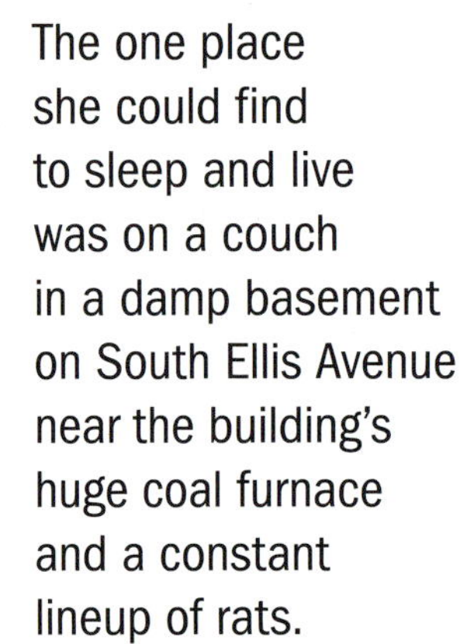

The one place
she could find
to sleep and live
was on a couch
in a damp basement
on South Ellis Avenue
near the building's
huge coal furnace
and a constant
lineup of rats.

Looking for ways
to take action in the city,
Grace signed up
with a local organization
of renters and workers.
Black people were fighting hard
for a fair share,
for their children
and the future,
though they were outnumbered
and outranked.
It was in Chicago
that Grace met
thinker, historian, and activist C. L. R. James,
and she caught his enthusiasm
for a new American revolution.

A PURPOSE

Spurred by the power
of Black folks struggling
and strategizing
and taking bold actions
to change
the whole country,

Grace joined the
South Side Tenants Union in Chicago.
She was about to learn something that would
change and forever guide her life.

War in Europe had broken out in 1939,
and white workers in the US got good jobs
in the defense industry
as the nation began sending supplies
to overseas allies.
Black people, who struggled
under Jim Crow discrimination,
were prevented from work and equal pay.
In Chicago, A. Philip Randolph,
a Black labor leader, ignited a mass movement
by calling for people to march on Washington
for equality in jobs.

The march was planned for July 1, 1941, and because of the thousands of people joining meetings and adding pressure for change, President Roosevelt eventually issued Executive Order 8802, which banned racial discrimination in defense jobs. Randolph called off the march.

Grace learned
that masses of people
organizing together
can bring about important change.
She had found
her calling
as an activist.

MOVEMENT

James joined
the union's
Fair Practice Committee
to get fair pay
and to open up all positions
to Black workers,
not just the most dangerous jobs.

James searched
for different points of view,
alternative ideas, and
new strategies
to improve the lives
of Black people
and all workers.

His head swirled
with what he learned.

After working all day
making sure his children
were fed and safe in bed,
James attended meetings
of the Communist Party,
the Socialist Workers Party,
the NAACP.

Ideas in the meetings
challenged
the way things were.
People used words like *revolution*
and proposed equal rights
for Black people.

When you have to fight
for the right
to vote and go to school
and eat and shop
and sit and drink
and love,

when you are threatened,
your family beaten,
your kin killed,
because of racism,
labels don't matter.
Ideas and actions do.

James worked with the NAACP
to see if hotels, bowling alleys, and stores
served factory workers like him,
forcing businesses
to comply with
antidiscrimination laws.

In another group,
James met people passionate about
making the world a better place:
C. L. R. James, Freddy and Lyman Paine,
and Grace Lee.

They started a newspaper
called *Correspondence*,
writing and publishing
FOR the workers,
giving them a voice—
a space on the printed page
to share their ideas
and vent their rage.
James was becoming
a thought leader.

FEARLESS

James had become
a husband and father.
Nothing stopped him
from moving forward.
Fearless

James sang to his baby boy
much of the night
so he wouldn't cry.
The landlord wouldn't care why—
crying babies got families evicted
when rooms for rent were hard to find.
Fearless

One sunny Sunday afternoon
after picnicking on beautiful Belle Isle,
James brought his family home
just before riots erupted.

Angry white workers
protested the promotion
of Black workers
to wartime production,
spilling hatred and blood
into neighborhoods.

Sitting on the porch
with his bride by his side
and their babies in their arms,
James was nearly shot
as a bullet flew
just over his head.
Fearless

James spoke his mind
at work,
at meetings,
at organizing conferences,
and even to the FBI
speaking truth
to power.
He wrote honestly
about history
and revolution
and living conditions,
criticizing so-called
leaders,
white and Black.
Fearless

GRACE AND JAMES

In 1953, Grace moved to Detroit,
known as Motor City,
to work on *Correspondence*
with James.

For her, James was
"a breath of fresh air."
When he opened his mouth,
truth tumbled out
along with Alabama.
He worked hard with his hands
at the factory
and at home with his kids
and at organizing meetings with his pen.

But Grace knew
he was going through hard times:
recently separated, soon to be divorced.
And he had no car
in Motor City.
Grace bought a 1938 red Plymouth
for $100.
She would drive James home
after meetings,
with him mostly quiet.

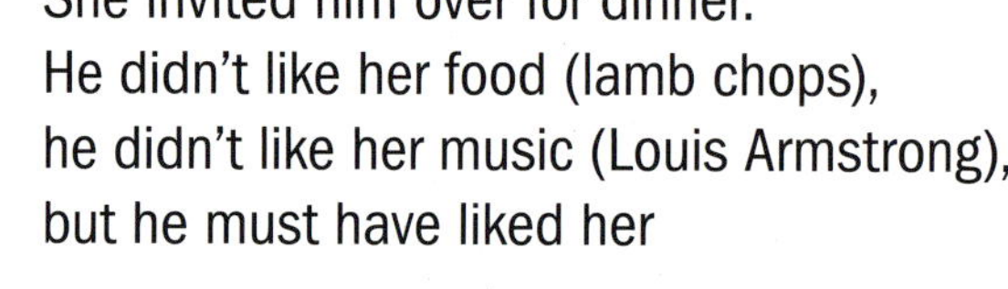

She invited him over for dinner.
He didn't like her food (lamb chops),
he didn't like her music (Louis Armstrong),
but he must have liked her

because later that night,
he asked her
to marry him,
and impressed by his ideas,
his energy, his fire,
she found herself saying
Yes.

IN LOVE AND STRUGGLE

It didn't matter that
James was Black *Grace was Chinese American*
James was from the country **Grace was from the city**
James had a high school diploma *Grace had a PhD*
their relationship
was illegal
in parts of the country.

Theirs was a true
collaboration,
a union
of love
and struggle.

DIALECTICAL CONVERSATION

Many people
talk the talk,
but do they walk the walk?
James and Grace walked the talk.

They believed
in the power of ideas,
talking about them,
and thinking through
everything.
They engaged in *dialectic*,
which means
the art of investigating
or discussing
the truth
of opinions.
They and their fellow
activists
knew that ideas
and action
have to go
hand in hand
to transform
society
as well as
ourselves.

ALSO KNOWN AS

He was born James Boggs
but answered to son and brother,
comrade and friend.
Listening to their problems,
showing up at the grocery store just
before closing
to buy fresh food at a bargain:
tomatoes, potatoes, onions—
food that hadn't sold
and would just get old,
he brought around to neighbors.

An arts lover,
James quoted poet
Countee Cullen,
read Richard Wright,
listened to Dinah Washington.
Their shared Southern roots
filled his soul
with the sights, sounds, and scents
of Black 'Bama.
Pride,
anchoring him to his people.

At home, after work at the factory,
James fixed a faucet
or cleaned the counter,
always thinking,
before
he lay on the
living room floor,
writing on yellow legal pads,
feeling the passion of purpose
pulse through his fingers
and out his pen.

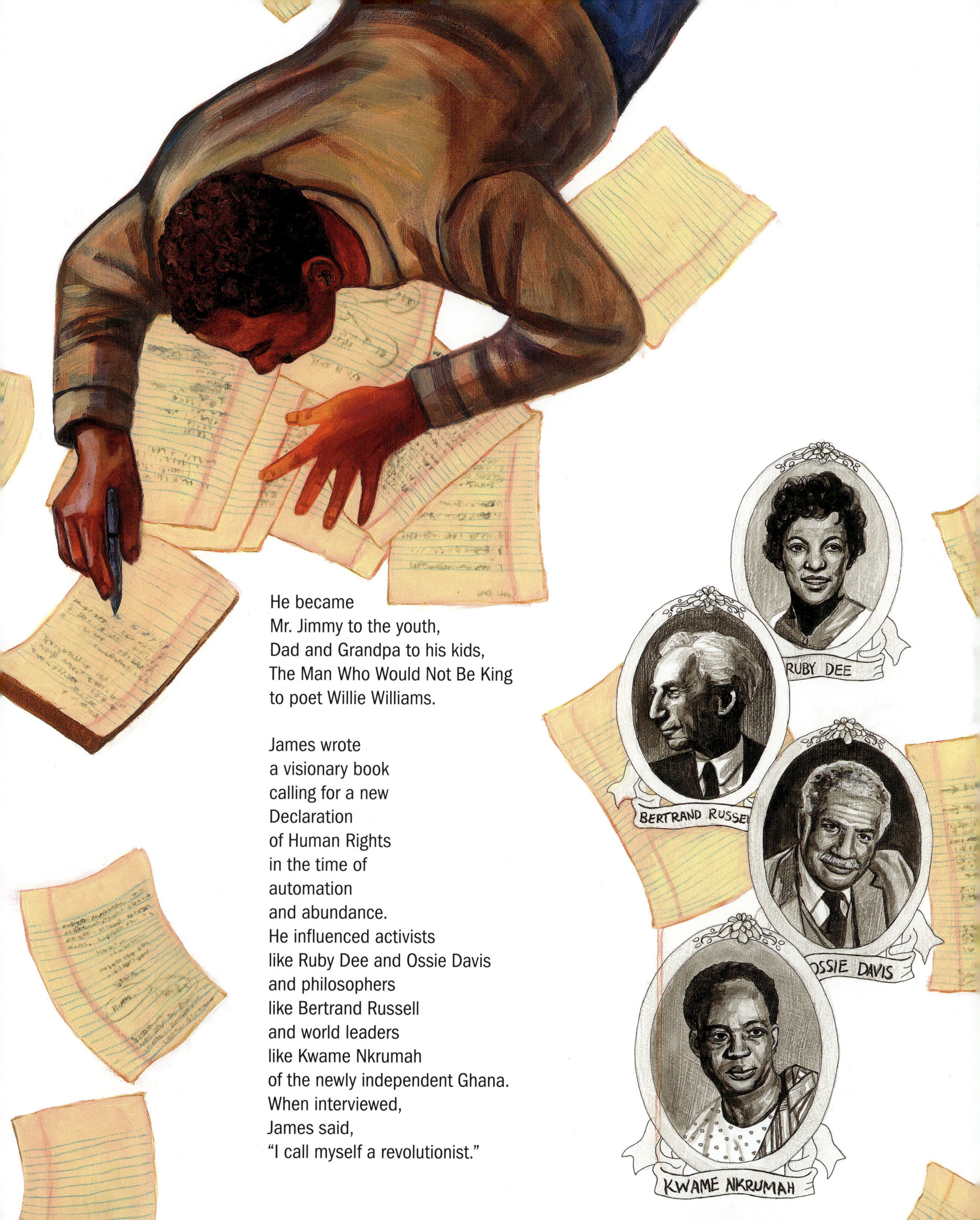

He became
Mr. Jimmy to the youth,
Dad and Grandpa to his kids,
The Man Who Would Not Be King
to poet Willie Williams.

James wrote
a visionary book
calling for a new
Declaration
of Human Rights
in the time of
automation
and abundance.
He influenced activists
like Ruby Dee and Ossie Davis
and philosophers
like Bertrand Russell
and world leaders
like Kwame Nkrumah
of the newly independent Ghana.
When interviewed,
James said,
"I call myself a revolutionist."

REVOLUTION

Grace believed that
revolution
meant
re-evolution
from the ground up
everyday people stepping up
to help each other
live consciously,
create compassionately,
grow and appreciate
nature, food, animals,
build community,
share knowledge,
repair bicycles,
plant vegetables,
read and think,
question and adapt
to
elevate
humanity
evolving
to
a higher level.

NEW DREAMS FOR THE TWENTY-FIRST CENTURY

In 1984, at the end of November
in the sleet
and rain,
tens of thousands of Detroiters
lined up
for food.
There weren't
enough
good jobs
for everyone.

Some of the young people,
impatient and hungry,
were shoving aside their elders.
Grace and James
brought a few of the older folks together
to demand
that Neighborhood Services
set aside a day
for the elderly
and disabled
to line up
in peace.
They called themselves
Detroiters for Dignity,
and they won
their special day.

DETRO
FOR
DIGNIT
FOOD FOR EVER

REBUILDING OUR CITIES

In 1992, Grace and James
sensed a new movement
to rebuild communities
was in the making.
They asked themselves
what they could do
to make a difference.
Inspired by
how Mississippi Freedom Summer
brought young people
from the North
to help
in the 1964 voter registration drive.

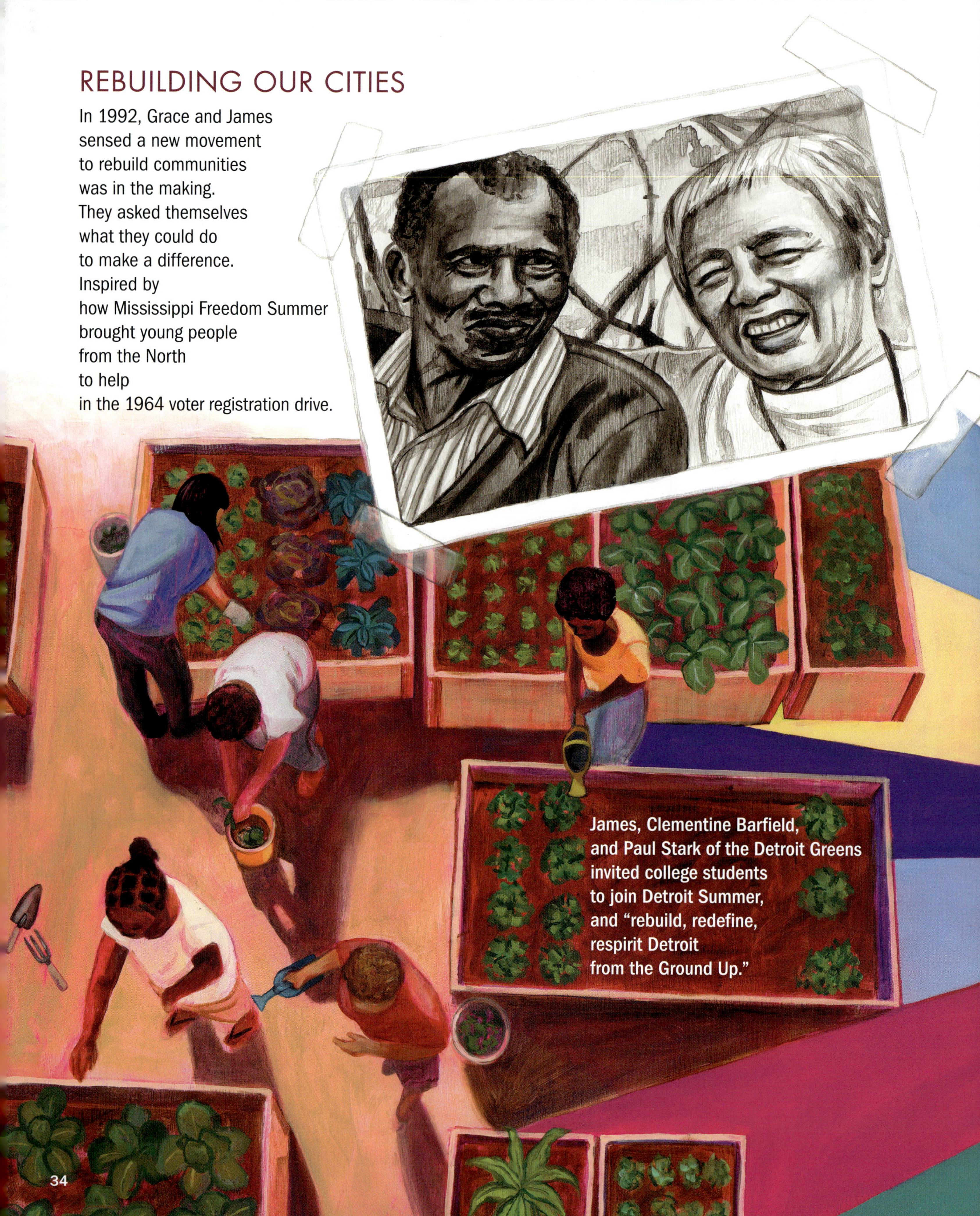

James, Clementine Barfield,
and Paul Stark of the Detroit Greens
invited college students
to join Detroit Summer,
and "rebuild, redefine,
respirit Detroit
from the Ground Up."

BEING PART OF THE SOLUTION

Tracey Hollins,
a teenage volunteer
wrote, "Detroit Summer
filled your head
with answers
to questions that you'd had
all your life . . .
It made you feel
you were an important part
of the changing
and molding
of future generations.
It made you feel
that the hole you dug,
the garden you watered
or the swing set you painted,
made a difference."

WHAT KIND OF WORLD DO WE WANT?

The James and Grace Lee Boggs Center
was born
at the same time
as Detroit Summer
out of this belief:
"Revolutions are made
out of love
for people
and for place."

James and Grace,
two very
different people
from very
different places—
Marion Junction, Alabama,
and Providence, Rhode Island—
made a life together:
full of
study,
gathering,
learning,
inspiration,
ideas,
writing,
sharing,
hope,
and meaning
by working
with others—
the old,
the young,
and everyone in between,
for a better future
for all.